HEALING - THE SHAMAN'S WAY
BOOK 4 - ESSENTIAL OILS

Norman W. Wilson PhD

HEALING - THE SHAMAN'S WAY
BOOK 4- ESSENTIAL OILS

Cover Design by

www.srwalkerdesigns.com

Interior Photography by
Suzanne V. Wilson Photography

A ZADKIEL PUBLISHING PAPERBACK

© Copyright 2023
Norman W. Wilson PhD

The right of Norman W. Wilson to be identified as author and channel of this work has been asserted by him in accordance with the Copyright, Designs and Patents Act 1988.

All Rights Reserved

No reproduction, copy or transmission of the publication may be made without written permission.

No paragraph of this publication may be reproduced, copied or transmitted save with the written permission of the publisher, or in accordance with the provisions of the Copyright Act 1956 (as amended).

Any person who does any unauthorised act in relation to this publication may be liable to criminal prosecution and civil claims for damages.

ISBN: 978-1-78695-855-6

Zadkiel Publishing
An Imprint of Fiction4All
www.fiction4all.com

This Edition
Published 2023

DISCLAIMER

Even though there is specific evidence about the use of essential oils by humankind, there is very little scientific medical evidence currently available to support healing claims. There is abundance of supportive testimonial evidence. If you are considering the use of essential oils for implied medical issues check with your medical doctor. Do not hesitate to do a patch test. Most essential oil should not be taken internally. Those that have been suggested as 'safe' to use internally are always done with water or an approved carrier oil.

Intention plays a hugely significant and important role is the success of any medical or supportive medicine use. Without a specific and positive intention, the chance for success is minimalized.

I acknowledge that some of the "success" credited to the use of essential oils may very well be the placebo effect. My professional attitude is "So what! If it works use it!"

Norman W. Wilson, PhD
Certified Aromatherapist Practitioner

A SPECIAL THANKS TO

Stuart Holland, my publisher, for his advice and personal care in the completion of this work, and bringing it to the printed page.

Stephen R Walker, my book cover designer, for his personal attention to the execution of design appropriate for the subject matter of my books.

Omar Lopes, PhD, my book's interior designer, for his keen insight in what photos, drawings, charts, and graphics best illustrates concepts presented in the textual content of the book.

Suzanne V Wilson, my wife, who has endured times of grumpiness, isolation, and cry for help when things were not going the way I thought they should.

CHAPTER ONE

GETTING STARTED

Essential oils have been around for a long time. Records from Ancient Egypt suggest the use of oils as early as 4500 BCE. From China comes *The Yellow Emperor's Book of Internal Medicine* (2697-2597 BCE) A translated copy of this ancient book is available.

When applied to plant medicine the word essential means any component necessary for the plant's survival. As far as oils are concerned essential means those part of a plant necessary to create an oil.

It is estimated there are 320,000 species of plants in existence today. Of these, an estimated 80,000 have medical value. This figure changes as scientist continue to test

Because of the proliferation of essential oils made available in a wide variety of stores, small shops, and on the internet, it strongly recommended that you make sure the oils you buy are as they are claimed to be. When buying any essential oil check the following factors:
1. Is the common and scientific name of the plant on the label?
2. Has the method of production been identified?
3. The color of the bottle should be dark blue, green, or amber. The bottle should be glass.
4. Is the part(s) of the plant used to create the oil identified?
5. Check certification: USDA Organic, PETA's & Cruelty-Free, Leaping-Bunny Cruelty-Free Certification and the non-GMO statement.

A story worth repeating

A number of years ago I visited a "metaphysical store" in a neighboring city. There, lined up on shelves were various bottles filled with essential oils. One caught my attention. The label boldly claimed Pure Essential Oil Moldavite. I thought this was a wonderful discovery since Moldavite comes from a meteorite that hit the earth millions of years ago. I bought it. Using a magnifying glass, I discovered a minuscule piece of Moldavite. Once I had the small bottle opened my nose was assaulted with a disgusting sweet smell—a carrier oil. The sweetened carrier oil was oil pure. The Moldavite had not been made into an essential oil. Buyer beware is a good motto to follow.

Essential oils are generally divided into two distinct groups of chemical constituents or parts: Hydrocarbons and Oxygenated Compounds. Included in the Hydrocarbons are terpenes which inhibit the accumulation of toxins and aid in the discharge of toxins from the liver and kidneys. The Oxygenated Compounds of essential oils include Esters. Esters are the result of reaction to alcohol with an acid. They are anti-fungal and help create a calming and relaxing sensation.

The smell of essential oils can trigger five different aspects of influence for an individual. Memories and feelings can be provoked by the smell of a particular essential oil. The five aspects of essential oil influence are:

1. May open a sense of personal inner peace that may result in improved self-esteem
2. Opens the potentiality of acknowledging both good and bad and still recognizing the value in any situation
3. Depending on the intensity of the essential oil's aroma, one's emotions and temperament may be impacted
4. May accelerate the healing of wounds
5. May open the individual to a new level of relaxation, allowing healing.

As with many things in life, there is a negative side to the use of essential oils. There are common irritants found in some of essential oils, especially those that are fragrant. These irritants include limonene, citronellol, eugenol, and linalool.

A basic rule of thumb for the use of essential oils is do not apply them directly to your skin. An exception is Frankincense Essential Oil. It may be applied around the outer edges of a wound that is not healing. This stops the spread of the infection and allows natural healing to take place. To help ensure the safe use of any essential oil it is highly recommended to do a patch test by applying a very small amount of an essential oil directly to the skin. If redness, swelling, or itching occurs stop using the oil. Wash the area with mild soap and warm water. It it doesn't clear up, consult your medical doctor. The same cautionary note applies to a spray, incense, or diffuser. Do a sniff test. If your eyes, nose or throat become irritated discontinue use.

What then, are essential oils? They are concentrated hydrophobic liquids. Generally, hydrophobic means a fear of water, but in chemistry, it refers to the property of a substance to repel water. These hydrophobic liquids are often called volatile or ethereal oils. Some believe that any essential oil that I created using chemical processes are not true essential oils. Essential oils are made from plants; more specifically, specialized plant cells that exist in minuscule sacs in the plants.

There are several methods of extracting oils from plants. Depending on your interests and needs extraction methods become important. There are nine extraction methods:
1. Steal Distillation
2. Absolutes
3. Mechanical
4. CO2
5. Cold Press
6. Water Distillation
7. Solvent Extraction
8. Enfleurage
9. Maceration

Of these nine extraction methods only these four will be discussed in detail: Steam Distillation, CO2 Extraction, Maceration, and Water Distillation.

Steam Distillation

The most popular method of creating essential oils is, without a doubt, steam distillation. It involves the following: A still is required. A still is an apparatus used to distill liquid mixtures by heating to selectively boil and then cooling to condense the vapor. Usually, the still is made of stainless steel. Plant materials are placed within the container which has an outlet for steam to flow to a condenser and on to a separator. Small stills for at home use can be purchased online for about $80. Large stills cost $1300 and up. Oil and water do not mix. As a consequence, oil floats to the top of the separator. It can, ten be siphoned off.

Some essential oils have a higher density than water. The density of a liquid is a measure of how heavy it is for the amount measured. High density fluids will sink to the bottom. Clove, Cinnamon, and Vetiver oils are heavier in density.

A major problem in using the Steam Distillation Method in creating essential oils is the quality of the oil varies. The reason for this is that much depends on the degree of temperatures, pressures, and time involved in the distillation process. Considerable damage to the oil can be caused by heat and thus reduces its effectiveness. There is a workable way around this issue. The CO_2 Extraction Method provides an answer.

CO_2 Extraction

Even though Steam Distillation is considered the most popular method of creating essential oils, CO_2 Extraction is viewed as producing a higher quality oil. The reason for this is the lack of high heat. For example, Steam Distillation heat ranges from 40 to 212 degrees F; whereas, CO_2 ranges rom 95 to 100 degrees F. The CO! oils are generally thicker than some of the other extraction processes, consequently, the aroma is more pronounced.

In this process, the carbon dioxide is pressurized and becomes liquid. It is then pumped into a container filled with plant matter. The liquid properties of the CO_2 function as a solvent. The plant materials' oils dissolve into liquid CO_2. It then, is brought back to a natural pressure and evaporates. What remains is the essential oil. A rewarding spin-off of the CO_2 process is that there are no harmful solvents to humans or to the environments. The diagram of the CO_2 process gives a graphic image of the procedure.

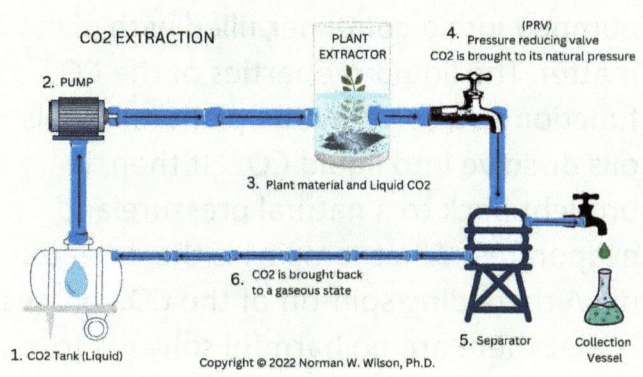

CO2 Extracted Oil

Maceration

Oils created using the Maceration process are referred to as *infused oils*. The Maceration method is the most used for removing the oils from certain flowers. The process involves soaking flower petals in warm fats (carrier oils). The essence of the flowers is drawn into the fat. Once removed, the fat is dissolved in alcohol so the extract of the floral oil can be used.

A chief benefit of Maceration is that more of a plant's essence is accumulated in the carrier oil. The heavier and larger molecules of the plants are captured. The Maceration Process involves the following:

- Very dry plant materials are ground into a medium coarse powder. If the plant material is not dry the moisture can cause the oil to become rancid. To discourage the potentiality of rancidity, Vitamin E or Wheatgerm Oil is added.

- The plant material is placed in a closed container
- Solvent is added.
- The plant material is shaken occasionally for one week
- The liquid is strained.
- The remaining solid is pressed to remove any remaining liquid
- The strained and the pressed liquids are mixed
- The liquid is clarified using a filtration process.
- The base oil will probably change color.
- The oil is placed in an airtight dark glass container and stored in a cool dry place for 12 months.

A diagram of the Maceration Process appears on the next page.

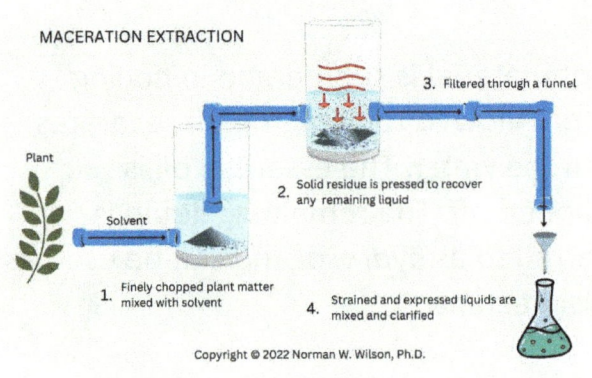

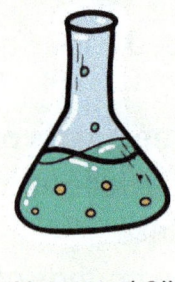

Macerated Oil

Many of the distillation methods of oil extraction are expensive and not practical for the do-it-yourself type person. There is hope. There is a method you can do at home that won't break the bank. It called Water Distillation.

Water Distillation

Plant material is submerged in boiling water. Allowed to gool, the oil separates from the water. The essential oil is siphoned off. The remaining liquid is referred to as *hydrosol* and can be used as a disinfectant.

How To Do It Yourself

- You will need a four-quart sterilized pot
- Two to three quarts of distilled water
- A grinder such as used for grinding coffee beans
- A good two pounds of plant material such as the flower petals of Rosemary, Lavender for example
- A sharp knife
- A clean sterilized dark glass bottle with cap

Directions

- Pour the water in the pot and bring it to a roaring boil

- While the water is coming to a boil, cut the stems from the flowers
- Add the flowers to the grinder. Set it for a coarse grind.
- Remove the pot of boiling water from the heat
- Add the ground flower mixture to the boiling water, making sure it is well submerged
- Let the mixture cool and then remove the solids
- Pour the remaining liquid into the bottle, cap it, and store in a cool, dark place.

A Water Distillation Chart on the next page show in diagram format the process.

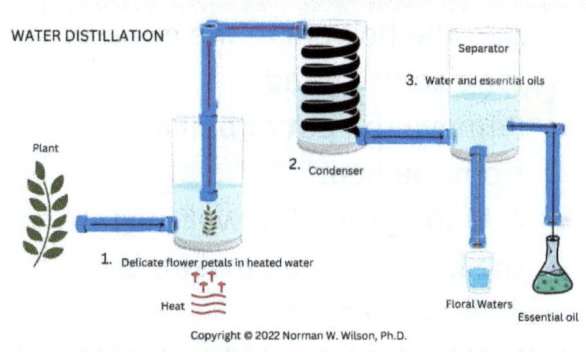

Water Distillation Oil

CARRIER OILS AND THEIR USES

Carrier Oils are associated with essential oils. What is a carrier oil or as it is sometimes called, base oil? Why are they strongly suggested for use with essential oils? Does their addition to the essential oil men the mixture is no longer "pure" essential oil?

A very mild oil used as a base for essential oils is called a *carrier oil*. Because some essential oils are so strong, they could harm your skin, a carrier oil is needed. A general recommendation is to NEVER place an essential directly on your skin without a patch test. If redness occurs consult with your medical doctor. Oregano is a good example of a strong essential oil that could burn your skin.

Carrier oils are also used during a treatment procedure called layering. This will be discussed later. For now, the recommended carrier oils include the following:

List of Carrier Oils

Borage Oil	Jojoba Oil
Walnut Oil	Macadamia Oil
Sweet Almond Oil	Rosehip Oil
Argan Oil	Fractionated Coconut Oil
Grapeseed Oil	Avocado Oil
Neem Oil	Castor Oil
Hemp Seed Oil	Olive Oil
Vitamin E Oil	Wheatgerm Oil

AVOIDING ISSUES WITH ESSENTIAL OILS

As with other things, you should avoid certain aspects of essential oils if you have allergies or are sensitive. For instance, some irritations are caused by fragrance ingredients. Among these are limonene, citronellol, eugenol, and linalool. All of these are found in many fragrant oils. The following chart shows which oils contain the potential irritant fragrance ingredients.

Oils Containing Fragrance Ingredients that may Irritate

Limonene	**Citronellol**
Eugenol	**Linalool**
Orange	Rose
Clove	Lavender
Grapefruit	Geranium
Cinnamon	Rose
Lemon	Lemongrass
Tulsi	Neroli

CHAPTER TWO

WORKING WITH ESSENTIAL OILS

PART ONE

As you continue this adventure in essential oils please keep in mind the following major points:

- Many claims for the successful uses of the proposed essential oil are strictly subjective
- Scientific proof of essential oils' effectiveness is not always readily available.
- The oils suggested in this lecture are by no means the

only oils that could be used for the specific suggested purposes.

Second, before using any of the suggested oils, be sure to do a patch test. If redness or skin irritation shows up, wash the area, and stop using that particular oil. Then consult your medical doctor to determine if they are safe for you to use. The following 6 essential oils will be discussed:

- Red Mandarin
- Silver Fir
- Helichrysum
- Ho Wood
- Holy Basil
- Black Spruce

<u>Red Mandarin</u>

It is a cold-pressed essential oil. Only the outer peel of the Mandarin fruit is used. It has a sweet yet tart aroma. As an additive to a diffuser, it radiates a pleasant smell throughout a room. In the United States, Red Mandarin is called Tangerine.

If you feel tired, lackluster, or malcontent mix 2 eyedroppers full of Red Mandarin with 4 eyedroppers full of carrier oil such as Jojoba. Place the mixture in a roll-on bottle. Shake it to ensure the oils are well mixed. Then, Rub the back of one wrist and gently rub your wrists together for a couple of seconds. You will soon begin to feel better.

If you are experiencing abdominal bloating, use the same blend as just described and rub it around your abdomen.

To help improve circulations using the roll-on, apply a small about to one wrist, and rub your wrists together. Do this just before going to bed and again in the morning.

If you want to kick things up a notch, Red Mandarin works well with the following essential oils: Holy Basil, Bergamot, Spikenard, and or Rosemary.

Silver Fir

Silver Fir is a steam-distilled essential oil. If you have cancer, epilepsy, or liver issues check with your medical doctor before using Silver Fir. It is not recommended for use if you are pregnant or to be applied to young children. The operative words here are *due diligence*.

Silver Fir Essential Oil helps with respiratory issues, bronchitis, colds, and the discomfort of the flu or Covid-19. Placing 5 drops in a diffuser will help lessen fatigue and sinusitis.

To help relieve muscular pain combine 4 drops of Silver Fir Essential Oil with 6 eyedroppers full of carrier oil. I recommend jojoba as the carrier oil because Silver Fir has a wonderful warm woodsy smell.

If you suffer from Seasonal affective disorder combine 3 drops of Silver Fir Essential Oil with Orange Essential Oil in a diffuser. There are small personal diffusers available that work well in a home office.

Helichrysum

Helichrysum is part of the Sunflower family. All parts of this plant are used to create an essential oil. Even the dried leaves are used for medicinal purposes. The smell of Helichrysum is that of light curry.

Because Helichrysum is anti-inflammatory, antifungal, and antibacterial it promotes healing, fights infections, and reduces inflammation. Additionally, it helps reduce the effects of allergies, the common cold, and associated coughs. Other issues to which Helichrysum may be applied include the following:

- Skin irritations
- Bloating
- Indigestion
- Acid Reflux

For skin irritation be sure to do a patch test first. If any redness shows up, check with your medical doctor before continuing. It's always better to be safe than sorry. If no problem is indicated follow these steps:

- Place two to three drops of Helichrysum in a tablespoon of carrier oil. I suggest Jojoba rather than one of the nut-based oils. It reduces the potential skin issue with Almond oils, for example. Gently rub a small amount on the skin once or twice a day for three days. If the irritation continues check with your dermatologist.

Ho Wood

Ho Wood is a camphor plant and its oil is made by the steam distillation process. The bark and wood are used to make the essential oil. Ho Wood's sweet woodsy smell help calm you. It helps relieve the following:

- Colds
- Flu
- Wounds
- Stress

- Mental instability

Additionally, Ho Wood Essential Oil boosts the immune system, eases headaches, and combats parasites and skin infections.

Ho Wood Essential Oil blends well with Clary Sage, Frankincense, and Lavender Essential oils.

HO WOOD RECIPE

INDUCING PEACEFUL THOUGHTS FOR POSITIVE DREAMS

<u>What you will need:</u>

- Ho Wood Essential Oil,
- Bergamot Essential Oil
- Juniper Essential Oil
- Mandarin Essential Oil
- One essential oil inhaler (Available on the Internet with prices ranging from $7 to $20)
- A pair of sterilized tweezers
- One ¼ oz measuring cup

If an inhaler is not readily available to you, use a cotton ball, or a small bottle, or a small dish.

<u>Directions</u>: Using a commercial inhaler

6 drops of jojoba carrier oil

Add three drops of each of these essential oils: Ho Wood, Bergamot, Juniper, and

Mandarin in a small sterilized dish. Mix well

Place the cotton wick insert that comes with the inhaler in the dish. Use the tweezers to make sure the wick is thoroughly saturated with the essential oil mixture.

Return the wick to the inhaler holder. Make sure the parts are closed tightly.

Close one nostril, hold the inhaler close to the open nostril and breathe in. Change nostrils and repeat. Do this twice a day, preferably at bedtime.

Shake the inhaler a couple of times before each use.

If you don't have an inhaler, use a small dish with the oil in it, hold it up to your nose, and inhale.

Holy Basil

Do not confuse Holy Basil with the garden variety that is used in cooking. Holy Basil is also called Tulsi. All parts of the plant are used. Each part, for example, may be used for a different issue. Research has shown that Holy Basil contains pharmacological properties that help in the following areas:

- Reducing and coping with stress
- Relieves sleep issues
- Reduces forgetfulness
- Other memory issues
- Helps repair ulcers
- Lowers blood sugar
- Lowers high cholesterol
- Releases intestinal gas
- Soothes sore muscles

Some people should avoid using Holy Basil. Among these are pregnant women and breastfeeding women. Those who are undergoing cancer treatment should refrain from using Holy Basil as well as those with serious skin disorders and heart issues. Always check with your medical doctor before embracing the use of essential oils.

A PATCH TEST FOR HOLY BASIL

Place one drop of Holy Basil and 4 drops of your carrier oil into a small dish. Mix thoroughly. Dip a finger into the mixture and place a small amount on your wrist. Check within 30 minutes. If there is a redness or any indication of skin irritation, thoroughly wash to the spot. Do not use Holy Basil until you check with your medical doctor.

HOLY BASIL RECIPE FOR SOOTHING SORE MUSCLES

At some time during your life, you will have had or will have sore muscles. Add 2 or 3 drops of Holy Basil in your favorite carrier oil. Gently massage the oil into the affected area. Just to rev it up a bit add this mixture to your bath water with two tablespoons of Epsom Salt.

Black Spruce

The needles and branches of the Picea Mariana Tree are distilled to create Black Spruce Essential Oil. Its natural woodsy aroma offers immediate comfort, something needed in today's topsy-turvy world.

Black Spruce Essential Oil helps restore and promote the following:

- Basic skin health
- Calmness
- Harmony and Balance in one's life
- Respiratory issues

- Immune System
- Reduce arthritis and gout pain
- Improved sleep
- Hair

RECIPE FOR SLEEP IMPROVEMENT

You will need:

- Black Spruce Essential Oil
- Cedarwood Essential Oil
- Frankincense Essential oil
- A diffuser
- Water

Direction:

- Place 5 drops of Black Spruce Essential Oil in the diffuser
- Add 5 drops of Cedarwood Essential Oil
- Add 5 drops of Frankincense Essential Oil
- Add water to the diffuser. Follow the directions that come with the diffuser.
- Place the diffuser in your bedroom and turn it on 20 minutes before

retiring. Leave it on until it automatically shuts down.

RECIPE FOR BEARD AND MUSTACHE

Men often have problems with growing and maintaining a beard and or mustache. Course beard and mustache are never attractive. All too often the skin beneath the beard is neglected and dandruff and other skin irritations result. Applying essential oils result in a softer beard and mustache, improved skin, and even hair growth.

<u>You Will Need:</u>

- 6 drops of Frankincense Essential Oil
- 8 drops of Black Spruce Essential Oil
- 5 drops of Cedarwood Essential Oil
- 5 drops of Bergamot Essential Oil
- 10 ml of Jojoba Oil

<u>Directions:</u>

- Combine the listed ingredients in a dark-colored bottle with a dropper
- Shake well to insure a good mix of the oils
- Add 1 to 2 drops (more if the beard is thick) of the mixture to the beard and gently massage.
- Do the same for the mustache.
- Apply once daily.

As this class ends, a gentle reminder: Keep all of your essential oils in a dark, low-heat, and dry place. Light changes the strength of the essential oil.

CHAPTER THREE

WORKING WITH ESSENTIAL OILS

PART TWO

Several processes for creating essential oils have been reviewed. Here is one you can do at home without the expensive equipment.

Cold Pressing

Orange Essential Oil makes a wonderfully soothing massage oil. It provides relief from pain and can be applied wherever there is pain. Here are the directions for making cold-pressed Orange Essential Oil:

What You Will Need:

- 25 to 35 large ripe oranges.

- ! paring knife
- 1 thermometer
- 1 pot for boiling water
- A juicer
- A ¼ measuring cup
- 1 small sterilized bottle with a stopper
- 1 juice pitcher
- 1 garlic press
- 4 to 6 ounces of Jojoba Oil

Directions:

1. Remove any stickers on the oranges. Clean the oranges with a cloth soaked in lavender hydrosol. Rinse. If you do not have the hydrosol, tap water will do just fine. Dry the oranges.
2. Peel each orange, laying aside.
3. Once the oranges are peeled, scrape away the white pith on each piece. Get it as pith clear as possible. The pith will absorb any of the juice.
4. Cut the orange peel into about one-inch pieces.

5. Place the orange slices in a pot, and add enough water to cover the slices.
6. Heat to 120 degrees. Test with the thermometer. Remove from heat and let it set for 10 minutes.
7. Remove enough of the orange peel to fill the press, and squeeze it into the measuring cup. Continue until all the orange peel has been used up.
8. Mix the orange oil with the Jojoba carrier oil. Place in the bottle with a topper.
9. Juice the oranges and refrigerate.
10. Discard the pulp.

Before using the Orange Essential Oil for a massage, hold the bottle in your hand for a couple of minutes, then shake the bottle to insure a good mix. Place a couple of drops of the oil where you are experiencing pain.

Petitgrain Essential Oil

Petitgrain Essential Oil is made from the Bitter Orange Tree. The twigs, leaves, and branches are steam distilled. Petitgrain blends well with other citrus and wood oils. Petitgrain Essential Oil is used to help with the following:

- Uplifts one's spirit
- Calming
- Balancing
- Easing anxiety
- Reducing insomnia
- Reducing stress
- Clearing up Acne and or oily skin

Petitgrain Essential Oil may be mixed with a carrier oil and applied to the skin. Remember to do a patch test first.

To help relieve stress rub a small amount on one wrist, and rub your wrists together for a couple of seconds. If you are stressed out and need quick relief from anxiety, use an inhaler and take two deep breaths through one nostril and repeat with the second nostril.

If you are experiencing a bout with insomnia add four drops of Petitgrain Essential Oil to your diffuser. Add water as per the diffuser's directions. Turn on the diffuser as you retire.

For relief from acne and or oily skin, mix two drops of the Petitgrain Essential Oil with 3 drops of Jojoba Oil and apply to the problem area of your skin. Wash your face with a bar of mild soap after 15 to 20 minutes.

Sunpati Essential Oil

<u>Sunpati Essential Oil</u> reportedly has the botanical name Rhododendron. It has a long history of being used for medicinal purposes as well as an herbal tea. Sunpati Essential Oil is created by distilling the flowers of the plant. It helps support the following:

- The Respiratory System
- Acts as a decongestant
- Relieves sore joints and aching muscles

Additionally, Sunpati Essential Oil helps with these issues:

- Eases tension
- Grounds for meditation
- Relaxes the whole body
- Induces sleep.

One of the most valuable qualities of Sunpati Essential Oil is it strengthens one's sense of security and empowerment.

RECIPE TO CALM, RELAX AND INDUCE SLEEP

<u>What You Will Need:</u>

One quality diffuser that has a timer

¼ to ½ cup of distilled water (tap water will work)

4 to 8 drops of Sunpati Essential Oil

Sunpati Essential Oil blends well with Clary Sage, Rose, Pine, Lemon, and Lavender. If you wish, reduce the amount of Sunpati by two drops and add one of these oils.

<u>Directions:</u>

Place the diffuser in your bedroom. Turn it on for 15 to 30 minutes before retiring.

RECIPE TO RELIEVE MUSCLE PAIN

1.7 billion people in the world suffer muscle pain. Lower back pain is the leading cause of disability in 160 countries. Essential Oils, less costly than many treatments, are a welcome trend. Sunpati helps relieve muscle pain.

<u>What You Will Need:</u>

- 4 to 5 drops of Sunpati Essential oil
- 2 drops of Clary Sage
- 8 drops of a carrier oil such as Jojoba Oil
- 1 small mixing bowl

<u>Directions:</u>

Thoroughly mix the oils. To increase their effectiveness, warm the oils. Be careful to not overheat.

Massage the warm oils into the muscles or lower back.

Rose Essential Oil

<u>Rose Essential Oil</u>

Rose Essential Oil is expensive and that is easily understood when you realize it takes 252,000 rose petals (that's 80,000 rose flowers) to make 5ml of essential oil. Pure essential oil and that is the only kind I use and recommend, is very potent. Because of that high potency Rose Essential Oil should never be applied directly to the skin. Always blend with a carrier oil.

Known for its antidepressant, antiseptic, and antispasmodic qualities, it is also known to help with hemostatic and neuro issues. The following chart, listing some of the benefits of Rose Essential Oil gives a broad picture of its many uses.

Rose Essential Oil may also help with these issues:

- Helps clear up Acne
- Scar issues

- Soothes skin irritations
- Reduces the size of pores
- Reduces anxiety, depression, and stress
- Reduces headache pain
- Relieves menstrual pain

As with other oils, there are some negative side effects to using Rose Essential Oil. Among these are nausea, vomiting, diarrhea, and or redness in the eyes. Rose Essential Oil should not be used during pregnancy. It could lead to a potential miscarriage or abnormal bleeding.

Using Rose Essential Oil for a bath and or foot soak can bring much-needed relief from stress and pain.

RECIPE FOR ROSE ESSENTIAL OIL BATH

What You Will Need

- Rose Essential Oil
- Carrier Oil of choice
- A large Turkish Bathe Towel or a Terry Cloth Robe

Directions:

- Mix 10 drops of Rose Essential Oil with 1 ounce of carrier oil.
- Draw hot water for your tube. Test for your comfort level
- Add the essential oil.
- Soak for 15 to 20 minutes.
- Upon exiting from the tub wrap yourself in the Turkish Bathe Towel or Terry Cloth Robe
- Sit or lay down for 10 to 20 minutes

RECIPE FOR ROSE ESSENTIAL OIL FOOT BATH

What You Will Need:

- A pan big enough to hold water and your feet
- Warm water to cover your feet
- A soft towel
- 10 drops of Rose Essential Oil
- 15 to 20 drops of carrier oil
- A chair or stool

Directions:

- Heat the water. Be careful not to make it too hot
- Mix the Rose Essential Oil and the carrier oil
- Add the oil mixture to the warm water, and stir around
- Test the water with a foot. If comfortable sit with both feet in the water for 10 to 15 minutes.

- To kick this up a notch, consider add 5 drops of Rosemary Essential Oil

Today's world produces a great deal of physical and emotional stress, anxiety, and depression. To avoid the endless drug treadmill consider using essential oils to combat the rigors of contemporary daily life. There are three ways to use Rose Essential Oil to help relieve anxiety, stress, and depression:

1. Massage
2. Inhaler
3. Diffuser

For a massage add 4 drops of Rose Essential Oil, 2 drops of Frankincense Essential oil to 10 drops of carrier oil.

Add 5 drops of Rose Essential Oil to an inhaler. If you don't have one, add it to a small plate, and inhale through one nostril at a time. Do this twice, wait 10 minutes, and repeat the process.

Add Rose Essential Oil to a diffuser, following the directions that come with the machine.

CREATING YOUR OWN ROSE ESSENTIAL OIL

You may choose to create your own Rose Essential Oil. If you do, here are the steps.

What You Will Need

- A large glass jar with a lid
- Rose petals
- Carrier oil
- Cheesecloth (or a very fine strainer)
- A dark-colored bottle with a rubber stopper

Directions:

- Collect roses from a fragrant bush in your garden. Separate the petals. Be sure they are pesticide free. Early morning is the recommended time for collecting the roses.

- This is a very important step. Use a screen (like those used for a window) and place the rose petals on the screen and set out in the sun to dry. This will eliminate the possibility of mold. If you don't have a screen readily available, use sheets of paper towels. Place a weight on each end of the towels to prevent them from being blown away.
- Be sure you have enough rose petals to fill your jar ¾ full. As you insert the rose petals, gently pack them down.
- Fill the glass jar with the carrier oil. Fill it to the top. Add the lid, making sure it is secure, and then vigorously shake the jar.
- Place the jar of rose petals in the sun and leave it there (bring it in at night) for 2 to 3 weeks. Shake the jar daily.

- At the end of two weeks, strain the oil through a cheesecloth or fine strainer. Throw away the petals. Place the remaining oil in a dark-colored bottle with a rubber stopper.

You can apply the Rose Essential Oil to your face, use it in a massage, or on your feet and hands. Remember, a carrier oil has been added; you are not using undiluted oil.

CHAPTER FOUR

WORING WITH ESSENTIAL OILS

PART 3

Over 21 billion dollars were spent on essential oils in 2022. Staggering as that figure is, it is predicted to far exceed that in 2023. From my perspective, the rapid continued use of essential oils as alternative medicine is alarming. Essential oils should never be used as a substitute for sound medical treatment. Many of the claims for the use of essential oils lack substantial research to back them up. Further, it has been charged that whatever effect essential oils may have, is simply the result of a placebo effect. I have said, if it works, who cares if it was placebo?

There are a few areas I wish to revisit. In previous lectures, I said certain oils blend well with others. Blending refers to mixing compatible oils for a specific purpose. Not all essential oils blend well together. (SEE RESOURCES for Complimentary Essential Oil Blending Chart)

To begin:

- Decide the issue(s) you want to relieve,
- Select the oils that address that specific issue.
- Check to see which oils blend to provide you with a broader healing base. +
- Do not apply essential oils directly to your skin. Use a carrier oil.

Applying an essential oil to your skin:

First, like most medicines, essential oils are not intended to stay in the body for prolonged periods. Consequently, your essential oil should be applied several times a day to be the most effective. It is suggested that when an essential oil is applied to the wrist it takes 20 seconds to enter the bloodstream. At the end of 20 minutes, it has traveled throughout the body and is being expelled. Please note that it may take longer. Each person reacts differently. Here is a short list of essential oils that have demonstrated skin-healing properties:

List of Essential Oils That Have Helped Skin Issues

Cedarwood   German Chamomile   Roman Chamomile

Frankincense   Geranium   Helichrysum

Jasmine   Lavender   Myrrh

Neroli   Patchouli   Rose

Sandalwood   Vetiver   Ylang-Ylang

Skin issues may be allergies based. Allergies are caused by a histamine response to a wide range of things including food, pollen, dust, environment, and pet dander. A negative reaction to any one of these including essential oils may result in diarrhea, swelling of the tongue, sneezing, labored breathing, or wheezing.

Several essential oils may be helpful in the treatment of allergies. Among these are the following:

ESSENTIAL OILS	ALLERGIES ISSUES
Elemi	psoriasis
Eucalyptus	Sinus, Asthma
Lavender	Respiratory
Ledum	Digestive
Lemon	Pollen, Molds
Melissa	Skin
Patchouli	Vomiting, cramps
Peppermint	Sinus
Spikenard	Sinus

Sometimes it is necessary to dilute essential oils used in massage therapy. The AIA (Alliance of International Aromatherapists) suggests 1 percent dilution equals 3 drops of essential oil per tablespoon of carrier oil. It provides the following guideline for diluting essential oils:

- 2 percent dilution for the average adult with no known issues
- 1 percent dilution for older adults (over 65)
- 1 percent dilution for children aged six
- 1 percent for pregnant women
- 1 percent for those who have compromised immune systems, health issues, and or skin that is sensitive

Limonene

Terpenes are the primary constituents of essential oils and in citrus fruits, the terpene is called Limonene. For a few years, many of those who are into personal health and fitness have been taking Limonene or eating more citrus. According to a review in PUB/MED GOV, "Therapeutic effects of limonene have been extensively studied, proving anti-inflammatory, antioxidant, antinociceptive, anticancer, antidiabetic, anti-hyperalgesic, antiviral, and gastroprotective effects, among other beneficial effects in health." (Vieira AJ, Beserra FP, Souza MC, Totti BM, Rozza AL. Limonene: Aroma of innovation in health and disease. Chem Biol Interact. 2018 Mar 1; 283:97-106. doi: 10.1016/j.cbi.2018.02.007. Epub 2018 Feb 7. PMID: 29427589.)

Just because Limonene has many health benefits doesn't mean that there aren't potential risks in using Limonene supplements. This is true for those who are into megadoses, that is, more than 8 grams per day. Nausea, vomiting, and skin irritations may occur. Women who are pregnant or breastfeeding should check with their medical doctor before using.

The suggested dosage of Limonene is about 2 grams per day.

<u>Layering Essential Oils</u>

Originally named Raindrop Therapy, or as it is sometimes called Raindrop Technique or Aroma Touch. It involves applying a specific number of drops of specific pure essential oils. That is, the oils are not mixed with a carrier oil. And therein, lies the issue. Aromatherapists DO NOT recommend the use of essential oils directly on the skin. Professional aromatherapist organizations have recommended not using Raindrop Therapy. The Alliance of International Aromatherapists is an example.

Another criticism leveled at Raindrop Therapy is that the entire procedure is enchased in unnecessary ceremonial procedures. I disagree with this criticism. Sometimes a little ceremony helps the client relax, and tune into the healing processes.

The 16th Century German proverb, "Don't throw out the baby with the bath water," is appropriate here. There isn't a rule that says one can't change the suggested essential oils. One should choose those oils that are more likely beneficial to the client. I recommend layering essential oils that have been mixed with a carrier oil. I generally use Jojoba Oil or Olive Oil because it eliminates the potential issue of allergies to nut-based oils. Remember to do a patch test first. Also, ask the client if there are any allergy issues to the oils you plan to use. Here is a suggested list of essential oils and the procedure for using them in a Layering Treatment.

SUGGESTED OILS FOR LAYERING

- Holy Basil   Wintergreen
  Marjoram   Cypress
  Thyme
- Peppermint Oregano
  Cedar Wood Lavender
  Ylang-ylang

Wintergreen has been criticized and has been suggested by some aromatherapists that it should not be used. However, research does show that wintergreen essential oil acts as a natural pain reducer.

(Hebert PR, Barice EJ, Hennekens CH. Treatment of low back pain: the potential clinical and public health benefits of topical herbal remedies. J Altern Complement Med. 2014 Apr;20(4):219-20. doi: 10.1089/acm.2013.0313. Epub 2013 Oct 11. PMID: 24116881; PMCID: PMC3995208.)

LAYERING TECHNIQUE FOR BACK PAIN OR SHOULDER PAIN

Check in terms of allergies to essential oils. Take time to do a sniff test to see if any of the following oils are a problem. If there is any question do a patch test. Wait 20 minutes and if there is any redness or developing rash, don't proceed using that oil.

<u>What You Will Need</u>

- 2 drops of Holy Basil Essential oil
- 3 drops of Wintergreen Essential Oil
- 2 drops of Marjoram Essential Oil
- 1 drop of Cyprus Essential Oil
- 1 drop of Thyme Essential Oil
- 2 drops of Peppermint Essential Oil
- 1 drop of Oregano Essential Oil
- 2 drops of Cedarwood Essential Oil
- 2 drops of Lavender Essential Oil
- 2 drops of Ylang-Ylang Essential oil
- 1 to 2 ounces of Jojoba Oil
- A sterilized dark brown bottle (large enough to hold the oils) with an eye dropper

- A large, warmed bath towel

Directions For Self-Application:

- Mix the oils thoroughly.
- Warm the towel.
- Place the warm towel over the shoulders, or lower back.
- Apply the essential oil mix but do not rub it in
- Wait 20 minutes and then shower. *

*NOTE: If you are an Essential Oils Practitioner make sure the client is comfortable on the massage table. Use a soft pillow to support the client's head. In place of the shower and Just before the end of the twenty minutes check to see if there are any remaining oils on the skin. If so, gently massage that area. Pat dry with a clean towel.

CHAPTER FIVE

SHAMANIC MEDITATION & ESSENTIAL OILS

Mindfulness allows us to become keen observers of ourselves and gradually transform the way our minds operate.
Mark W. Muesse, Ph.D.

Actual records of the early use of any form of meditation are scarce. There is some indication that meditation was a part of early forms of the Vedic Religion out of what is now called Iran. An estimated date is 1500 BCE.

The Chinese Taoists, as well as the Indian Buddhists, began to develop versions of meditation practices during the 6th Century BCE. (Before the Current Era) Whatever its origin, the many forms of meditation complicate the historical perspective.

Meditation piqued the Western mind in the 1700s CE (Current Era) as some Eastern philosophy books were translated into European languages. These texts referenced meditation techniques. International interest in meditation is primarily credited to the presence of Swami Vivekananda.

In 1893, he was a key presenter at the Parliament of Religions held in Chicago. Over the years, his talk influenced other well-known Indian religious teachers to come to the United States. Among these were Swami Rama, Mukunda Lal Ghosh, and Maharishi Mahesh Yogi. During the 20th century, mediation took on a significant role in people's daily lives. This was especially true for the United States

Nine popular types of meditation practice include the following:

- mindfulness meditation.
- spiritual meditation.
- focused meditation.
- movement meditation.

- mantra meditation.
- transcendental meditation.
- progressive relaxation.
- loving-kindness meditation.

Of these 9, Mindfulness Meditation will serve as an example.

<u>Mindfulness</u>

The basic idea of Mindfulness dates back to 1500 BCE in India and the Hindu practice of yoga. Yoga back then was more involved in stillness and breathing rather than movement as it is today. Breathing and stillness of both body and mind hold center stage in Mindfulness.

Jon Kabat-Zinn founded the Stress Reduction Clinic at the University of Massachusetts Medical School in the 1970s. Mindfulness, as do other forms of meditation, reduces stress, anxiety, and depression. It also is helpful for those who are dealing with the myriad mental and emotional issues of daily life.

The three principles of Mindfulness Meditation are:

- Setting the intention to cultivate awareness
- Pay attention to what is going on in the present moment and do so simply as an observer
- Have a non-judgmental attitude.

On a brief personal note, I began my meditation practice following Maharishi Mahesh Yogi and then the teachings of the late Allan Watts. Eventually, I moved into Mindful Meditation with Mark W. Muesse whose technique is heavily influenced by Vipassana Meditation, one of India's oldest methods of meditation.

Certainly, one of the most important things you learn through meditation is an awareness of breathing. Such a focus helps you develop a better understanding of your body. Its use will help calm you, relax you, and most likely prolong your life.

My purpose here is not to teach you Mindful Meditation, but to lay the groundwork for Shamanic Meditation. Admittedly, I begin with a ten-minute warm-up using Mindful Meditation.

In Shamanism there are two distinct meditation methods: Shamanic Meditation and Shamanic Journeying. Each has its singular purpose. Shamanic Meditation's main purpose is to re-energize the individual; whereas, Shamanic Journeying's purpose is to connect to the Spirit World.

<u>Shamanic Meditation</u>

Traditional healers often meditated outside allowing the natural world's rhythmic dance to lead them to a quiet time. For most people that is not possible in today's hectic world. Please keep in mind that Shamanic Meditation is supposed to be a heightened state of presence . . . that eternal now.

During the Shamanic Mediation do not concentrate on one thought, that is, do not develop it. The goal is not to empty the mind but to quiet the mind.

Here are the steps for doing Shamanic Meditation:

<u>Getting Ready:</u>

If it is not comfortable to be in the yoga seated position, choose a chair in which you are comfortable. I do not recommend lying down because you are more apt to go to sleep.

Select a room in which you can lower the lights and close the shades. A dimly lighted room works fine. I do not recommend total darkness unless you plan to retire for the night.

Choose a sound to listen to as you meditate. Something quiet or a low steady drum beat. There are several excellent MP3 files available on the Internet. Piano and flute offer up quiet tones.

The selection of an essential oil for use in a diffuser is crucial. You should select something that not overpowering.

Consider cedarwood, cypress, and or lavender. Add 5 drops to the diffuser. Follow the directions that come with the diffuser.

<u>The Steps:</u>

1. Once you have completed the preceding items, place your hands, and palms up on your lap. Connect your index finger to your thumb on each hand.
2. Take 5 slow Ujjayi breaths
3. Set your intention (See Resources for a discussion about intention)
4. Take 5 slow Ujjayi breaths

Breathe normally. Relax your body.

5. At the end of 10 to 15 minutes, slowly get up, and gently stretch your arms above your head.
6. Drink some water.

A gentle reminder: Practice makes perfect.

Note: I have declined to teach Shamanic Journeying online because of the potential danger of a student not completely coming out of the trance state. However, I am rethinking that issue with the advent of live broadcasting. I am considering offering a certificated course for those who which to become Shamanic Practitioners. Namaste

CHAPTER SIX

ESSENTIAL OILS FOR THE BEDROOM

So far, I have dealt with two prominent methods of using essential oils: Topical Application and Inhalation.

Recently. there has been a spate of interest in a potential third use of essential oils, ingestion. The ingestion of essential oils is very **dangerous** and can result in death. Don't ingest pure essential oils. Reduce with water. It is important to keep this in mind as you continue to learn about the various uses of essential oils. This holds, especially for those that are used to alter one's mood.

Mood is a specific conscious state of mind. It is a predominant emotion or feeling. The 8 basic emotions are shown in the following chart.

I think there should be another and that is sexual desire. Sexual dysfunctions are highly prevalent, affecting about 43% of women and 31% of men. Erectile Dysfunction is experienced by most men by the age of 45. Further, the current prediction is that by 2025, 322 million men worldwide will be affected. The annual cost is over two billion dollars. There are several types of treatment including drugs. But what do you do if drugs are not a financial option or of interest to you?

What do you do when things are not quite right? Intimacy is not as it used to be. Essential oils can be of help. The following

6 essential oils build and rebuild those personal intimate feelings for women and those men who are experiencing erectile dysfunction.

- Catuaba
- Clary Sage
- Davana
- Neroli
- Patchouli
- Ylang-ylang

<u>Catuaba</u>

Coming from the bark of trees in the Brazilian Rainforest, Catuaba is said to stimulate the nervous system which may result in penile erection. Besides being an aphrodisiac, Catuaba is used for the following issues:

- Anxiety
- Asthma
- Bacterial infections
- Bronchitis
- Depression
- Fatigue

- Insomnia
- Memory problems

Catuaba is available in capsule form, as an extract, as powders, and as bark. The dosage depends on the manufacturer and ranges from 375 to 475 mg. Do not exceed the recommendation. Catuaba Bark is wildcrafted. The chips and shreds are used for making teas. Please note that the wildcrafted bark means it has not been sanitized. If you choose to use the raw bark, be sure you use boiling water and let the bark steep for a good 15 minutes.

There are possible negative side effects from using Catuaba such as headaches, sweating, dizziness, rapid heart rate, and priapism. Because there is the potential for impaired fertility women should not use Catuaba. Do not give Catuaba to children!

Clary Sage

Clary Sage is not the same as the sage used for culinary purposes. Its smell is delicate woodsy and slightly floral. The oil is extracted from the leaves and flower buds of the plant. The preferred source for this oil is France. The soil impacts all plants. The soil along the Mediterranean Basin seems to produce high-quality Clary Sage. Known as "The Woman's Oil," Clary Sage Essential Oil has multiple uses. Among these are the following:

- Reduces stress
- Heals skin wounds
- Relieves depression
- Reduces hot flashes
- Reduces menstrual cramps
- Boosts the libido

<u>How to Use Clary Sage Essential Oil</u>

First, make sure you do not apply the oil directly to the skin. Add the Clary to carrier oil. Do not place Clary Sage Essential Oil directly into your eyes, nostrils, or mouth. Do a patch test and if a problem is indicated check with your medical doctor before continuing use.

- Open the bottle of Clary Sage Essential Oil, hold it up to your nose, and breathe in. Do this several times. This will help calm you.
- Put 3 to 5 drops in a spray bottle, and add I cup of water. Spritz it around a room. Shake the spray bottle several times.
- Using the created spray, spritz your bedding a couple of times. Do the same for closets.
- Add 2 to 3 drops to carrier oil and gently massage your feet to help reduce hot flashes associated with menopause
- To reduce menstrual cramps, add 3 to 5 drops of Clary Essential Oil to 10 to 15 drops of carrier oil. Warm this and gently apply it to your abdomen. Do this daily.
- Add 3 to 5 drops of Clary Sage Essential Oil to the carrier oil of choice. Shake it to insure a good mixture. Add a drop or two to your wrist and rub them together. Add

one drop to the back of each ear to help reduce tension.

Caution: People with low blood pressure should not use Clary Essential Oil.

<u>Davana Essential Oil</u>

Native to India, the Davana Plant is a member of the daisy family. Created by the steam distillation method, Davana's warm woodsy sweet exotic aroma becomes paramount. Its many uses include the following:

- Fights bacterial infection
- Relieves bronchial congestion
- Helps calm a nervous stomach
- Relieves menstrual cramps
- Relieves anxiety, stress, and tension
- Reduces skin blemishes
- Acts as an aphrodisiac

To help enhance the romance in your life follow these directions:

- Create a massage:
    Combine 12 drops of Davana Essential Oil and 1 oz of carrier oil.

Have your partner massage your shoulders and back to help set the mood and stir up arousal.

- Set the mood:
  Add 4 drops of Davana Essential Oil to a diffuser

- Apply Davana Essential Oil to your body:
  Add 2 to 4 drops of Davana Essential Oil to your carrier oil
  Mix thoroughly
  Place one drop behind each ear and one drop at your neckline

Neroli Essential Oil

French Orange Blossoms are steam distilled to create Neroli Essential Oil. Neroli Essential Oil is an antidepressant, aphrodisiac, and antiseptic. It is considered to have a positive impact on the following:

- Soothing the nervous system
- Releases tension

- Relieves anxiety
- Increases circulation
- Uplifts mood
- Increases libido
- Reduces frigidity
- Helps cure erectile dysfunction

To enhance your love life, try these approaches:

- Aromatherapy- Place 3 to 4 drops of Neroli Essential Oil in a diffuser and set it going 20 minutes before going to bed
- Massage- Add 3 to 4 drops of Neroli Essential Oil to 8oz of Sweet Almond Oil (or another carrier oil of your choice). Thoroughly mix. Warm just a little.
Begin a slow circular massage on your partner.

<u>Patchouli Essential Oil</u>

Using the distillation process the Patchouli Essential Oil is made from the dried leaves of the Patchouli Plant. It has many uses including the following:

- Treatment for dermatitis, acne, and dry skin
- Eases the symptoms of colds, headaches, and stomach issues
- Relieves depression
- Eases stress and anxiety
- Controlling appetite
- Gives the libido a boost

To help with skin issues apply 1-2 drops of Patchouli Essential Oil in a carrier oil such as Sweet Almond Oil and apply for dry skin. For acne, add 1-2 drops of Patchouli Essential Oil into a carrier oil such as Grapeseed Oil and dab it on the acne.

Patchouli Essential Oil has been used for many years to give the libido a boost. It does this by stimulating estrogen and testosterone and at the same time, lessening sexual anxiety. To use Patchouli Essential Oil as an aphrodisiac, combine 1 to 2 drops into a carrier oil. Hempseed Oil is recommended because it is a thick oil. Give your partner a massage.

Patchouli Essential Oil is generally safe. Remember to do a patch test first. Never apply undiluted oil to your skin. If used in a diffuser be sure the area is well-ventilated. Headache, nausea, and even dizziness could occur. That would be self-defeating. Do not apply to young children.

Ylang-ylang

Ylang-ylang Essential Oil is made by distillation of the flowers from the Ylang-ylang tree. It is often called the *flower of flowers*. It is estimated that 200 pounds of flowers will make one liter of essential oil. The many uses for Ylang-ylang include the following:

- Encourages self-esteem,
- Calms
- Releases anger
- Relieves tension
- Soothes the skin
- Moisturizes hair

Ylang-ylang is recognized as one of the most powerful aphrodisiacs. It increases libido and physical attraction between lovers. It energizes and encourages circulation.

Recipe for a Ylang-ylang Sensual Massage

<u>What You Will Need:</u>

- Ylang-ylang Essential Oil
- Sandalwood Essential Oil
- Jasmine Gradiflorum Absolute
- Your preferred Carrier Oil
- 1 sterilized small glass bottle
- 1 sterilized eyedropper

<u>Directions:</u>

Using the sterilized eyedropper:

- add 4 drops of Ylang-ylang to the bottle
- add 4 drops of Sandalwood
- add 3 drops of Jasmine Grandiflorum Absolute

- add 2 fluid ounces of your carrier oil (Coconut Oil makes a nice complimentary carrier oil)
- Place the lid on the bottle, and shake well

Slightly warm the bottle so the oil is warm. Pour a few drops in the palm of one hand, rub your hands together, and apply to the desired areas for massaging.

CHAPTER SEVEN

OTHER GOOD USES FOR ESSENTIAL OILS

Using essential oils often requires the blending with carrier oils. The following chart created by Melody Joy Elick will save you hours of tedious research.

Essential Oil Complimentary Blending Chart

Essential Oil	Note	Blends well with...
Basil	Top	Bergamot, Black Pepper, Clary sage, Cedarwood, Eucalyptus, Coriander, Cypress
Bergamot	Top	Basil, Black Pepper, Cardamom, Cedarwood, Cinnamon, Clary Sage, CloveBud, Coriander, Cypress, Frankincense, Geranium, Grapefruit, Helichrysum, Jasmine, Lavender, Lemongrass, Lime, Marjoram, Orange, Patchouli,

		Rosemary, Ylang-Ylang
Black Pepper	Middle	Bergamot, Cardamom, Clary Sage, Fennel, Frankincense, Geranium, Grapefruit, Helichrysum, Lavender, Marjoram, Orange, Rosemary, Sandalwood, Tangerine, Ylang-Ylang
Chamomile Roman	Middle	Geranium, Grapefruit, Lavender, Lemongrass, Lime, Marjoram, Orange, Patchouli, Ylang-Ylang
Cardamom	Middle	Bergamot, Black Pepper, Cedarwood, Cinnamon, Clove Bud, Coriander, Douglas Fir, Fennel, Frankincense, Ginger, Grapefruit, Helichrysum, Jasmine, Lemongrass, Lime, Orange, Patchouli, Rose, Sandalwood, Ylang Ylang
Cassia	Top	Clove Bud, Coriander, Cardamom, Frankincense, Ginger, Grapefruit, Helichrysum, Lavender, Orange,

		Rosemary
Cedarwood	Base	Bergamot, Cardamom, Cassia, Clary Sage, Cypress, Douglas Fir, Eucalyptus, Fennel, Frankincense, Geranium, Grapefruit, Jasmine, Lavender, Marjoram, Orange, Rosemary, Sandalwood, Ylang-Ylang
Cinnamon	Base	Bergamot, Cardamom, Clove Bud, Coriander, Frankincense, Geranium Ginger, Grapefruit, Helichrysum, Lavender, Lemongrass, Marjoram, Orange, Patchouli, Rose, Tangerine, Ylang-Ylang
Clary Sage	Middle	Bergamot, Black Pepper, Cardamom, Cedarwood, Coriander, Cypress,

		Frankincense, Geranium, Grapefruit, Helichrysum, Jasmine, Lavender, Lime, Melaleuca, Orange, Patchouli, Rose, Sandalwood, Tangerine, and Ylang-Ylang, Vetiver
Clove Bud	Middle	Basil, Bergamot, Chamomile Roman, Cinnamon, Clary Sage, Geranium, Ginger, Grapefruit, Helichrysum, Jasmine, Lavender, Lime, Orange, Rose, Sandalwood, Tangerine, Ylang-Ylang, Vetiver
Coriander	Middle	Bergamot, Black Pepper, Cardamom, Cassia, Clary Sage, Cinnamon, Clove, Douglas Fir, Frankincense, Ginger, Grapefruit, Lavender, Lemongrass, Lime, Orange, Patchouli, Vetiver

Cypress	Middle	Bergamot, Cardamom, Cedarwood, Chamomile Roman, Clary Sage, Eucalyptus, Frankincense, Geranium, Lavender, Lime, Marjoram, Melaleuca, Orange, Rosemary, Sandalwood
Douglas Fir	Middle	Cardamom, Cedarwood, Eucalyptus, Frankincense, Lavender, Marjoram, Rosemary, Wintergreen, Vetiver
Eucalyptus	Top	Basil, Cedarwood, Clary Sage, Cypress, Douglas Fir, Geranium, Ginger, Lavender, Peppermint, Rosemary, Vetiver
Fennel	Top	Black Pepper, Cardamom, Cedarwood, Ginger, Lavender, Orange
Frankincense	Base	Basil, Bergamot, Black Pepper, Cinnamon, Clary Sage, Coriander, Cypress, Douglas Fir, Geranium, Cedarwood, Grapefruit, Lavender, Lime, Orange, Patchouli, Rose,

		Sandalwood, Tangerine, Ylang Ylang, Vetiver
Geranium	Middle	Basil, Bergamot, Black Pepper, Chamomile Roman, Clary sage, Clove Bud, Cypress, Frankincense, Ginger, Grapefruit, Jasmine, Lime, Orange, Patchouli, Peppermint, Rose, Rosemary, Sandalwood, Ylang Ylang, Vetiver
Ginger	Base	Bergamot, Cedarwood, Cinnamon, Clove bud, Eucalyptus, Fennel, Frankincense, Geranium, Grapefruit, Jasmine, Lime, Orange, Patchouli, Rose, Sandalwood, Ylang Ylang, Vetiver
Grapefruit	Top	Bergamot, Cedarwood, Chamomile Roman, Cinnamon, Clove Bud, Eucalyptus, Frankincense, Geranium, Grapefruit,

		Jasmine, Lime, Orange, Patchouli, Peppermint, Rosemary, Tangerine, Ylang Ylang
Helichrysum	Middle	Bergamot, Black Pepper, Cardamom, Cassia, Cinnamon, Clove Bud, Clary Sage, Lavender, Lime, Lemongrass, Orange, Rose, Ylang Ylang, Vetiver
Jasmine	Middle	Bergamot, Clary Sage, Clove Bud, Ginger, Grapefruit, Orange, Patchouli, Rose, Sandalwood, Tangerine, Ylang Ylang, Vetiver
Lavender	Top	Bergamot, Black Pepper, Cedarwood, Chamomile Roman, Clary Sage, Douglas Fir, Fennel, Frankincense, Geranium, Grapefruit, Helichrysum, Lemongrass, Lime, Orange, Peppermint, Rosemary, Ylang Ylang, Vetiver
Lemongrass	Top	Bergamot, Black Pepper, Cedarwood, Chamomile Roman, Clary Sage, Cypress,

		Geranium, Ginger, Grapefruit, Lavender, Melaleuca, Orange,Patchouli, Rosemary, Ylang Ylang, Vetiver
Lime	Top	Bergamot, Chamomile Roman, Clary sage, Geranium, Lavender, Marjoram, Rosemary, Tangerine, Wintergreen, Ylang Ylang, Vetiver
Marjoram	Top	Bergamot, Black Pepper, Cedarwood, Chamomile Roman, Cypress, Eucalyptus, Douglas Fir, Lavender, Lime, Melaleuca, Orange, Peppermint, Vetiver
Melaleuca	Middle	Bergamot, Black Pepper, Clary sage, Clove Bud, Cypress, Eucalyptus, Douglas Fir, Geranium, Lavender, Peppermint, Rosemary
Orange	Top	Bergamot, Black Pepper, Chamomile Roman, Cinnamon, Clary Sage, Clove Bud, Eucalyptus,

		Fennel, Frankincense, Geranium, Ginger, Grapefruit, Helichrysum, Jasmine, Lavender, Lime, Marjoram, Patchouli, Rose, Sandalwood, Ylang Ylang, Vetiver
Oregano	Middle	Bergamot, Cedarwood, Cypress, Eucalyptus, Douglas Fir, Geranium, Lavender, Lime, Melaleuca, Orange, Rosemary
Patchouli	Base	Bergamot, Black Pepper, Cedarwood, Chamomile Roman, Cinnamon,Clary Sage, Clove Bud, Frankincense, Geranium, Ginger, Grapefruit, Jasmine, Lavender, Lemongrass, Orange, Rose, Sandalwood, Tangerine
Peppermint	Top	Bergamot, Black Pepper, Cedarwood, Cypress, Eucalyptus, Douglas Fir,Geranium, Grapefruit, Lavender, Marjoram, Melaleuca, Rosemary,

		Wintergreen
Rosemary	Middle	Bergamot, Black Pepper, Cedarwood, Cinnamon, Clary Sage, Eucalyptus, Douglas Fir, Frankincense, Geranium, grapefruit, Lavender, Lime, Marjoram, Melaleuca, Peppermint
Rose	Middle	Bergamot, Clary Sage, Geranium, Helichrysum, Jasmine, Lavender, Orange, Patchouli, Sandalwood, Tangerine, Ylang Ylang, Vetiver
Sandalwood	Base	Bergamot, Black Pepper, Clary Sage, Clove Bud, Geranium, Grapefruit, frankincense, Jasmine, Lavender, Orange, Patchouli, Rose, Tangerine, Ylang Ylang, Vetiver
Spearmint	Top	Basil, Eucalyptus, Jasmine, Peppermint, Rosemary

Tangerine	Top	Bergamot, Black Pepper, Cinnamon, Clary Sage, Clove Bud, Frankincense, Geranium, Grapefruit, Jasmine, Lime, Patchouli, Rose, Sandalwood, Ylang Ylang, Vetiver
Wintergreen	Middle	Douglas Fir, Lime, Peppermint
Ylang Ylang	Middle	Bergamot, Black Pepper, Cedarwood, Chamomile Roman, Cinnamon, Clary Sage, Clove Bud, Eucalyptus, Geranium, Ginger, Grapefruit, Helichrysum, Jasmine, Lavender, Lemongrass, Lime, Orange, Patchouli, Rose, Sandalwood, Tangerine, Vetiver
Vetiver	Base	Black Pepper, Cardamom, Cassia, Cedarwood, Cinnamon, Clary Sage, Clove Bud, Coriander, Douglas Fir, Eucalyptus, Frankincense, Geranium, Helichrysum,

		Lavender, Marjoram, Jasmine, Sandalwood, Ylang-Ylang

NOTE. Permission for use granted by Melody Joy Elick 02/18/2023

CHAPTER EIGHT

ESSENTIAL OILS FOR ALOPECIA AREATA HAIR LOSS AND NEUROPAHY

What is Alopecia Areata? It's a disease that occurs when one's immune system attacks the hair follicles which causes hair loss. Nearly 8 million American suffer this disease. Of the worlds nearly 8 billion people, 2% are affected by this disease. People with these autoimmune disease are prone to getting Alopecia: psoriasis, thyroid disease, and or vitiligo.

Alopecia varies from person to person with some having issues at various times throughout their lives. As of this writing, there is no cure, but there are things one can do to help control and lessen the impact of this disease. Below is a chart of essential oils that help hair loss.

RECOMMENDED ESSENTAIL OILS FOR ALOPECIA AND GENERAL HAIR LOSS

Black Pepper Cedarwood
Clary Sage   Clove   Cypress

Frankincense Geranium
    Chamomile   Ginger
    Lavender

Lemon   Mastic
Palmarosa   Rosemary
Rosewood

Sage   Sandalwood
    Spikenard   Thyme
Ylang-ylang

RECIPES FOR ALOPECIA AND HAIR LOSS

Recipe #1

What You Will Need

1 60ml (3 oz) dark colored glass bottle with stopper

20 drops Cedarwood

20 drops Lavender

20 drops Thyme

20 drops Rosemary

Enough Carrier Oil to fill the bottle, leaving room for the stopper. (Choose one from the list provided)

Directions:

Use a sterilized bottle and eyedropper

Add the above ingredient to the bottle. Insert the dropper and make sure it is tight.

Gently shake the bottle to thoroughly mix the essential oils.

Apply 2 to 4 drop of the essential oil to the area of hair loss and gently massage into to the scalp. Best to do this a night. In the morning, using a mild shampoo, wash your hair. Do this three times a week for three week. Take a week off. Begin again. Continue this routine until the hair growth meets your satisfaction. Later on, you may have to repeat this process.

Recipe#2

What You Will Need

1 small dark colored glass bottle with a eyedropper

Carrier Oil of choice

Frankincense essential oil

Cypress essential oil

Geranium essential oil

Rosemary essential oil

Thyme essential oil

Directions

Add 20 drops of chosen carrier oil to the bottle

3 drops of Frankincense essential oil

3 drops of Cypress essential oil

3 drops of Geranium essential oil

3 Drops of Rosemary essential oil

3 drops of Thyme essential oil

Place the eyedropper back in the bottle, make sure the cap is tight. Shake well, apply 2 drops to the scalp where there is hair loss and gently massage. Do this at bed time. Shampoo the next morning using a very mild shampoo. Do this every night for 3 to 4 weeks. Take a week off and then begin the regimen over again until you are satisfied with the results.

NEUROPATHY AND ESSENTIAL OILS

Neuropathy occurs when your nerves stop working the way they should. Nerve cells may have been damaged or even destroyed. It may show itself in the form of pain, tingling, weakness in your feet, legs, and or hands. You may notice a change in the way you walk. An interesting side note involves those persons who have diabetes. Anywhere from 60% to 70% of those who suffer diabetes get neuropathy.

What causes neuropathy? Among the more common causes are these eight:

1. Autoimmune diseases
2. Diabetes
3. Infections
4. Inherited
5. Tumors
6. Bone marrow problems
7. Vitamin B12 deficiency
8. Excessive Vitamin B6

What is offered here is not a replacement for traditional medical treatment. It is strictly supportive and should be attempted only with your medical doctor's approval. The following 10 essential oils are highly recommended as oils that provide relief: Bergamot, Cinnamon, Eucalyptus, Geranium, Ginger, Holy Basil, Lavender, Lemongrass, Peppermint, and

Tea Tree. Bergamot, Cinnamon, Eucalyptus and Lavender will be discussed. Their recipes are applicable to remaining six oils.

Bergamot Essential Oil

Bergamot Essential Oil is made from Bergamot Oranges, an extremely sour fruit. As a result, it is seldom if ever just eaten. In addition to being used to make an essential oil, the peel of the orange is used to flavor foods, marmalades, alcohol drinks, and the Earl Grey Tea.

Bergamot Essential Oil is antiseptic, antispasmodic, and analgesic. It is its analgesic quality that provides relief from neuropathy pain. Bergamot Essential Oil should never be applied directly to the skin. Always use a carrier oil. Jojoba is probably the most popular. Jojoba oil, which is actually more of a wax than a liquid, is extracted from the seeds of the jojoba bush. It is about 54% wax. Do not ingest Jojoba Oil.

Recipe Bergamot Essential Oil

In a dark green, blue, or red glass bottle add 20 drops of Bergamot Essential Oil. Next add 4 ounces of a carrier oil of your choice. Close the bottle with its cap and sake to make sure the ingredients are well mixed. If you use Jojoba oil, remember is is mostly wax and it will harden in kept in a cool place. In that case, rinse the bottle in warm water for a few seconds.

Cinnamon Essential Oil

Cinnamon oil is obtained from the dried inner bark of the shoots of the topped Cinnamomum *zeylanicum tree*. It is indigenous to Sri Lanka and the Malabar Coast of India. It is also found in Jamaica and Brazil. The trees are topped is to induce the formation of shoots. The trees are allowed to grow further unless they turn to a uniform brown by formation of cork. There are two distinct types of cinnamon oil that is used: the oil made from the cinnamon leaf and the oil made from cinnamon bark. Both work to relieve leg and feet cramps. Neuropathy pain, arthritis pain, and menstrual cramps.

Because Cinnamon Essential Oil is strong never apply it directly to the skin. Always mix it with a carrier oil. Use caution when using Cinnamon Bark oil. It is known to be toxic and can cause issues.

The chart on the following page shows the types of pain cinnamon helps relieve including Neuropathy.

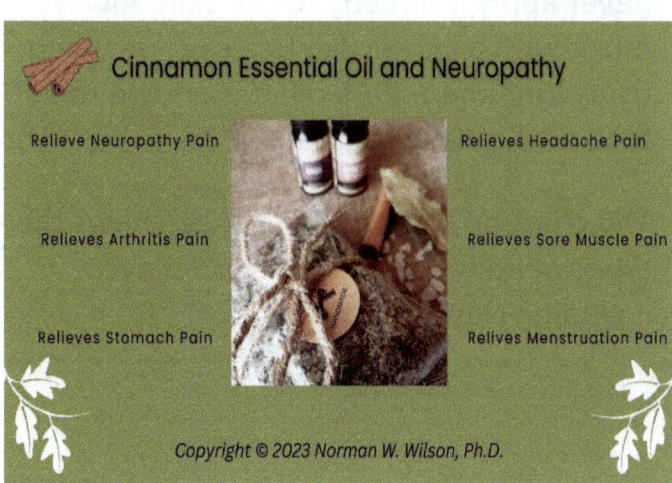

Cinnamon Essential Oil and Neuropathy

Relieve Neuropathy Pain

Relieves Arthritis Pain

Relieves Stomach Pain

Relieves Headache Pain

Relieves Sore Muscle Pain

Relives Menstruation Pain

Copyright © 2023 Norman W. Wilson, Ph.D.

Recipe for Cinnamon Essential Oil for Neuropathy

Using a 6-ounce dark colored glass bottle (one that has been sterilized) add the following:

    10 drops of pure Cinnamon Leaf Essential oil

    Fill the bottle with a carrier oil of your choice.

    Seal the bottle, shake well to insure a complete mix.

    Place a couple drops on your fingers and gently rub the oil into the area of pain.

*Because Cinnamon Essential Oil has a very strong aroma, you may want to add 5 drops of Lavender Essential Oil.

Eucalyptus Essential Oil

Now grown all over the world, Eucalyptus trees were once native only Australia. The tree's leaves are first dried and then crushed. A distillation process is used to release the oil from the leaves. Once extracted, the oil is then diluted so it can be used for medicinal purpose.

Eucalyptus Essential Oil has many medicinal purposes. Among these are coughing, gets rid of mucus, repels bugs, disinfect wounds, soothes col sores, and eases joint pain. When mixed with a carrier oil, Eucalyptus brings relief to pain caused by Neuropathy.

Recipe for Eucalyptus Essential Oil for Neuropathy

You will need 1 sterilized dark colored glass bottle with a stopper. Always store your essential oils in dark colored glass bottles. Light and heat tend to weaken essential oils' effectiveness.

To the glass bottle add 15 drops of Eucalyptus Essential Oil. Next add the carrier oil of choice. Add enough to nearly fill the bottle leaving enough room for the stopper. Tighten the stopper and shake the bottle until the oils are thoroughly mixed.

Place a couple of drops in one hand and gently apply to the leg. Do this daily.

You will most likely have to create more of the mixture. It is actually a good idea not to create a large quantity for a couple of reasons: You may not get the desired effect and you may not be consistent with the application and the oil turns old.

<u>Lavender Essential Oil</u>

Lavender Essential Oil is believed by many to be one of the best anti-pain oils. Lavender does promote sleep and a sense of relaxation. Its anti-inflammatory qualities help relieve neuropathy pain. Besides that, it smells good and promotes a sense of feeling good.

Add 10 drops of Lavender Essential Oil to two ounces of carrier oil. Make sure the oils are thoroughly mixed. Place a couple of drops in your hand and gently massage it on your effected leg.

CHAPTER NINE

ESSENTIAL OILS FOR VERTIGO

It is estimated that 40% of adults in the United States suffer vertigo at least once. With the current population of the United States of 332 million it readily is seen that 40 percent is a large number of people.

Recognized as an inner disorder in he 1860s by a French doctor named Prosper Meniere. (Pronounced men-EARS) His last name became the technical name for the inner ear issue we now call Vertigo.

Vertigo is described as dizziness, as being unsteady or having balance issues. It is caused by an inner ear infection. Vestibular neuritis may start after having a cold. It affects people differently and ranges from mild o severe. Symptoms may include a sensation of pressure in the ears, migraine headaches, sweating, nausea, vomiting, anxiety, and uncontrollable jerking (Nystagmus).

However, neuro-otologist Dr. Diego Kaski claims that the general descriptors of Vertigo may be mislabeled. It is likely to be benign paroxysmal positional vertigo. Benign paroxysmal positional vertigo (BPPV) is triggered by certain changes in head position, such as tipping the head up or down. Vestibular migraine causes episodes of dizziness described as rocking, spinning, floating, swaying, internal motion, and lightheadedness. Vertigo does not cause loss of consciousness. It can lead to falls and injuries.

Basically, BPPV is an inner ear mechanical problem. The inner ear contains crystals in its balance organs. These move when we do and if these get their signals mixed up and creates the illusion of physical movement. A head and neck adjustment may be required to get the crystals back in sync. It is not recommended that you attempt such an adjustment.

The three types of Vertigo are objective vertigo, , subjective vertigo and rotational vertigo.

- Objective Vertigo includes the sensation that the environment is in motion
- Subjective Vertigo includes the sensation that the individual is in motion
- Rotational Vertigo includes the sensation of spinning.

What can you do? Medical doctors may prescribe specific drugs, may recommend a change in diet and or exercise. Fortunately, there are several essential oils that help reduce the negative impact of vertigo.

Before using any of the following essential oils for vertigo you should check with your medical doctor. The old saying "It's better to play it safe than be sorry" holds true today as it did in years gone by. The following essential oils are recognized as effective in both the treatment and prevention of vertigo.

- Ginger Essential Oil is effective when it has been mixed with a carrier oil or used in a diffuser. Add 5 drops of Ginger Essential Oil to 2 ounces of carrier oil. Thoroughly mix and then gently apply a small amount to your temples, to your chest and back of your neck. Add 3 drops to a diffuser and sit nearby and slowly breath in and out.
- Cypress Essential oil increases blood flow resulting in improved brain functions. The increased blood flow makes light-headedness or dizziness less likely to occur. Add 3 to 5 drops to a room diffuser or to pot of boiling water to make steam inhalation. Breath this in for about 5 to 6 minutes. Add 5 drops to two ounces of carrier oil and at night before retiring, use it as chest rub.
- Basil Essential Oil placed in an inhaler or diffuser brings relief from the symptoms of vertigo. While the basil infused inhaler or diffuser brings relief, its anti-inflammatory

and antioxidant compounds help balance the nerves and as a consequence, calms the mind. To use Basil Essential Oil with an inhaler, add 2 to 3 drops to its inside. Add up to 5 drops in a diffuser. Follow the directions that come with the diffuser.
- Eucalyptus Essential Oil in an inhaler or diffuser helps reduce sinus pressure. Mixed with carrier oil Eucalyptus Essential Oil can be applied directly to the skin (chest, temples, forehead).

Other essential oils that help reduce the impact of vertigo include Clary Sage, Frankincense, Rosemary, Lavender, Peppermint and Rose Oil.

CHAPTER TEN

THOSE PESKY VEINS

Spider veins, or thread veins, as they are sometimes called, are smaller than varicose veins and effect the capillaries, the smallest blood vessels of the body. They are usually red.; they can be purple. They may look like branches of trees or spider webs. Spider veins can usually be seen under the skin, but they do not make the skin bulge out like varicose veins do. They may appear on the face as well as legs.

Spider veins may be caused by long hours of standing, obesity, and conditions that cause increased pressure in the abdomen such as constipation, too tight garments, trauma to the skin, and or exposure to ultraviolet rays.
Spider veins appear more often in women than in men. They may appear on the face.

What treatments are available?
Compression stockings is an immediate

and often comforting treatment. They come in three styles: below-the knee-, above-the-knee, and pantyhose. Sclerotherapy, Endovenous laser ablation, Radiofrequency Occlusion, Laser and Intense Pulsed Light, Surgery and Essential Oils.

Essential Oils for Spider Veins

lavender, horse chestnut, sea pine, mastic, grape vine, and yarrow are helpful oils in the treatment of Spider Veins. In addition to these oils, lemongrass and tea tree oils are recommended for facial Spider Veins. Horse chestnut and mastic essential oils serve as recipe examples.

Horse Chestnut Essential Oil

Horse chestnut is a tree native to parts of southeastern Europe. Its fruits contain seeds that resemble sweet chestnuts but have a bitter taste. Originally horse chestnut seed extract was used for joint pain, bladder and gastrointestinal problems, fever, and leg cramps. Today, however, it is used to relieve chronic venous insufficiency and poor blood circulation in the legs and facial veins.

As with all essential oils, do not apply directly to the skin. Be sure to do a patch test and consult your medical doctor before applying any oils to your face.

Here is a suggested recipe for Horse Chestnut Essential Oil for Spider Veins that can be applied to both the face and legs. You will need the following:

    1 two-ounce bottle of Horse Chestnut Essential Oil.

    1 three-ounce dark sterilized glass bottle with stopper

    3 to 4 drops of Horse Chestnut Essential Oil

    2 to 3-onces of carrier oil (You may want to not use Sweet Almond Oil, or Macadamia Oil, or Walnut Oil if you tend to have allergy issues with nuts. Avocado Oil is a good carrier oil to use.

Once the ingredients are in the dark glass bottle, insert the stoper, and sake well. Sake the bottle each time you use it. Place 1 or 2 drops on a finger and gently massage the oil into the Spider Vein area.

Do this daily and just before going to bed. The Spider Veins should be less pronounced within 5 days.

Mastic Essential Oil

Mastic Essential Oil's country of origin is Corsica. It is a considered to be a lymphatic and circulatory decongestant. Its constricting properties makes it an excellent oil to use for Spider Veins. The fact that it has an anti-inflammatory effect makes it an even stronger candidate for relieving Spider Veins. It blends well with these essential oils: Ambrette, Angelica, Balsam of Peru, Black Pepper, Chamomile and Cypress.

Mastic Essential Oil Recipe for use on Spider Veins.

5 drops of MEO (Masti Essential Oil)
2 ounces of carrier oil
Mix thoroughly.
Apply a small amount to the impacted veins. Gently massage the oil into the skin.

Re peat a couple times a day for two weeks. If improvement is not shown discontinue use.

VARICOSE VEINS

Varicose Veins are enlarged veins that are twisted like a cord in the calves of the legs. It is estimated that nearly 50% of adults develop varicose veins. Fortunately, they rarely cause serious health issues.

Most people assume varicose veins occur in the legs. They can appear anywhere on the body. Hemorrhoids are a form of varicose veins. An individual may have more than one varicose vein and they may not be the same size. Six of common symptoms of varicose veins include the following:

- The vein(s) may be bluish, purplish, or pinkish in color
- Aching legs
- Itching or the appearance of a rash near the affected vein
- A bulging or twisted vein showing just beneath the skin

- Soreness near the vein
- A mild bruising near the vein.

If you gently press on a varicose vein, it will feel soft. Normally there should be no pain and no change in its size. Complications can occur. These would include

- Hematoma, a large area of bruising or bleeding just beneath the skin
- Ulceration, an open wound that doesn't heal
- Phlebitis, an infection in the vein
- Thrombophlebitis, blood clots in the vein or an infection.

If you experience any one of the above you might have one or more of these complications: fever, redness and swelling of a vein, pain in the vein. If you do, consult your medial doctor.

There are things you can do besides surgery to reduce pain, redness, and general appearance of varicose veins. surgery. Among these are ice packs, massage, and essential oils.

ESSENTIAL OILS FOR VARICOSE VEINS

The same oils suggested for Spider Veins work well with Varicose Veins. Two of those, Grape Vine Essential Oil and Yarrow Essential Oil are presented here.

<u>Grapeseed Essential Oil</u>
Grapeseed Essential Oil is made from the left-over seeds of grapes used in creating wine. It is an excellent lubricant. To make a massage for varicose veins follow these simple steps:
- 5 ounces of carrier oil
- 8 drops of Grapeseed Essential Oil
- 6 drops of Frankincense Essential Oil
- 5 drops of Rosemary Essential Oil

Mix thoroughly. Place a few drops on your fingers and gently massage the area of the varicose veins. Leave on overnight. Wash the leg(s) with a mildly warm water and soap or shower down. Do this for 7 days. If no results show, discontinue use.

Yarrow Essential Oil

This oil is extracted from the yarrow plant which is related to chrysanthemums. It's flowers, leaves, and stems are used to make essential oil. Besides being an essential oil, yarrow may have the following forms: dried or fresh herb, capsules, tablets, and tinctures. To make a massage oil for varicose veins follow these directions:

- 5 ounces of carrier oil
- 6 drops of yarrow essential oil
- 3 drops of vetiver
- 2 drops of cedarwood

Thoroughly mix these 4 ingredients. Do a patch test on one wrist. If there is not issue then follow these directions. It's always a good idea to check with your medical doctor beforehand.

 Place a few drops in one hand and gently rub it over the area of varicose veins. Do this at night before retiring and do this for a week. If no results show, discontinue use.

Yarrow by itself may cause some issues such as skin irritation, drying of skin, and allergies.

CHAPTER ELEVEN

THE HYPOTHALAMUS, THYROID AND ESSENTIAL OILS

The Hypothalamus is a structure deep within your brain and it is about the size of a pearl. It's the main link between one's endocrine system and one's nervous system. It is the area of the brain that produce hormones. These hormones control body temperature, heart rate and one's hunger. It controls messages sent to and from the thyroid. This feedback loop is called the Hypothalamic-Pituitary-Thyroid Axis.

Chronic stress disrupts its ability to send and receive vital signals to the Thyroid. This throws everything within the body off balance. Health issues result—physical, mental, and emotional.

There are five highly recommended essential oils that ease stress which allows the hypothalamus to balance: Frankincense, Mandarin, Patchouli, Pine, and Ylang-Ylang. Suggestions for the use of these essential oil include a roll-on bottle or a spray. Both can use the same mixture of oils and carrier oil. Roll-on and spray bottles can be purchased from the Internet. If you do not have these five oils and can only get one, I suggest you buy pure Frankincense Essential Oil. Yes, it is the Frankincense from early Christianity.

Essential Oil Recipe for Hypothalamus

For a Roll-On Bottle use all 5 of the essential oils suggested. Here are the proportions:
- 5 drops of Frankincense Essential Oil
- 2 drops of Mandarin Essential Oil
- 2 drops of Patchouli Essential Oil
- 3 drops of Pine Essential Oil
- 2 drops of Ylang-Ylang Essential Oil

- 20 drops of carrier oil (Consider Sweet Almond Oils)

Insert the roller ball, place the cap on and check that it is on tight. Shake well. Roll four times at the Third Eye (The point just above the nose and between the eyebrows). Using your first finger, gently massage that area to work the oils into the skin. Do this daily. Preferably at bed time. Before giving the recipe for the spray bottle please note you do not have to use all of the 5 suggested oil. You can use just one.

- Add 5 drops of Frankincense to 20 drops of carrier oil.
- Thoroughly mix
- Spray a small amount on one hand, gently rub it in the middle of the forehead. Do this daily just before going to bed.

The Thyroid is a small gland. It is located in the front of the throat just below the Adam's apple and above one's collarbone. The thyroid regulates the rate the body converts oxygen and food into energy for the cells. The technical name for this wonderful process is *metabolism.* The two types of thyroid conditions are *Hypothyroidism* and *Hyperthyroidism*. Both have their own symptoms. The American Thyroid Association estimates there are some 20 million Americans that experience some type of thyroid disease.

Hypothyroidism:

Common symptoms of Hypothyroidism
- Cold hands and feet
- Constipation
- Difficulty in losing weight
- Fatigue easily
- Heavy menstrual periods
- Lack of initiative
- Sleepiness after having good night's sleep

Essential Oils for Hypothyroidism
- Clove
- Ledum
- Myrrh
- Peppermint
- Rose geranium
- Cedarwood

Ledum Essential Oil comes from leaves of the ledum plant. This plant has two common names: Greenland Moss or Labrador Tea. Ledum is one of those plants whose medicinal uses and benefits have been appreciated for hundreds of years. Ledum is recommended for those who suffer hyperthyroidism. It helps regulate hormone levels and thus ensures your body's metabolic functions are healthy.

Recommended Dosage of Essential Oils for Hypothyroidism

Remember do not take any essential oil orally without a carrier oil, tea, or water. It is always a good idea use oils for specific areas of concern that can only be met by ingesting the essential oil.

Generally, 1 drop of any of the suggested oils for Hypothyroidism is sufficient.
1 drop of oil to a cup of hot tea
Add 1 drop to a teaspoon of honey. Once in the mouth, turn the spoon upside down and lick it clean. This is to avoid getting any

of the oil on your lips which could cause some irritation.
Add 1 drop of oil to a piece of toast.
Add 1 drop to ¼ glass of water.

Consult your medical doctor before undertaking the use of any of the suggested essential oil for thyroid issues to make sure there isn't a conflict with your medical treatment.

Hyperthyroidism:

The condition in which your body produces too much of the thyroid hormone is called Hyperthyroidism. Symptoms include weight loss, irregular heartbeat, muscle weakness and the thyroid gland may feel inflamed. Hyperthyroidism can cause the thyroid gland to enlarge and form a goiter which can impact one's ability to breathe and swallow.

Essential oils can't stop the over-production of thyroid hormone. It is, however, believed that they can improve the symptoms of hyperthyroidism. The six recommended essential oils to be used to help hyperthyroidism are Lemongrass, Frankincense, Lavender, Wintergreen, Sandalwood, and Pine.

The procedures for using essential oils discussed under Hypothyroidism apply to the use of oils for Hyperthyroidism as well.

CHAPTER TWELVE

ESSENTIAL OILS FOR CONSTIPATION AND FLATULENCE

Constipation:

It is estimated that over 4 million people in the United States suffer from constipation and it is the most common digestive complaint. Over two million doctor visits annually are because of this uncomfortable condition. Constipation is that condition when one experiences infrequent bowel movements or the excrement is hard.

Hard, dry stool is the result of the colon's malfunctioning, that is, it is absorbing too much water. It may seem to be a contradiction to often given advice "drink more water" but it is not. The colon's muscle contractions are too slow and as a consequence, the stool moves too slowly through the colon. This results in too much water being absorbed.

Constipation may be caused by any one or number of the following:
- Lack of suitable exercise
- Not enough liquids
- Not enough fiber
- Intestinal malfunction
- Laxative abuse
- Medications
- Irritable bowel syndrome

The symptoms of constipation include the following:
- Difficult bowel movement
- Painful bowel movement
- Being bloated
- Being sluggish, lacking energy
- Cramps

Treatment for constipation depends on one's health. It may include a change in diet, specific exercise, and or medications.

ESSENTIAL OILS FOR CONSTIPATION

It is a given that essential oils have different effects on different people. If one oils doesn't work, try another. Before using any essential oil on your body, do a patch test. If there is any redness, itching, burning, or swelling immediately wash the area with a mild soap and warm water. Consult your medical doctor before continuing to use any essential oil.

The following essential oils are recommended for helping relieve issues associated with constipation:

- Ginger Essential Oil has long been used to settle an upset stomach. To help relieve constipation add 3 to 5 drops of Ginger Essential Oil to 1 full ounce of carrier oil. Thoroughly mix, place a couple of drops in your hand and gently massage the oil on your abdomen. Do this 3 or more times a day as needed.
- Helichrysum Essential Oil can be used to ease constipation. Add 2 drops of the oil to one teaspoon of carrier oil (Consider Sweet Almond oil). Mix thoroughly. Slight warm this mixture. Gently massage the oil onto your abdomen

and lower stomach area. Do this after your morning shower and again before retiring.

- Fennel Essential Oil is an effective relief for constipation. Mix 3 drops to one ounce of carrier oil. Mix thoroughly and rub onto the abdomen 2 or 3 times a day.
- Peppermint Essential Oil is well known as an aid for the relieve of stomach upset. Because it helps relax the muscles in the digestive tract, it loosens the bowels which in turn relieves constipation. Combine 2 to 3 drops of Peppermint Essential Oil with 1 tablespoon of warmed carrier oil (Avocado Oil or Olive Oil). Massage into the stomach and lower abdomen. Do this 2 to 3 times a day until the constipation is relieved.

These essential oils may also be used to help relieve constipation: Rosemary Essential Oil and Lemon Essential Oil.

Flatulence

Often the cause of embarrassment and hilarity flatulence, farting as it is commonly called, is simply the buildup of gas in the intestinal tract. There are several essential oils that can be applied to the stomach and lower abdomen that help relieve the buildup of gas. Among these are Angelica Root, Cardamom, Caraway, Coriander, Fennel, Lavender, Lemongrass, Peppermint, and Spearmint. For illustration purposes three oil recipes is given. For those oils not selected, follow the basic recipe procedure. You may need to experiment a bit to find out the dosage.

ESSENTIAL OILS FOR FLATULENCE

<u>Angelica Root Essential Oil</u>
　　　Add 3 to 5 drops of Angelica Root Essential Oil to 1 tablespoon of warmed carrier oil. Mix well and apply to the lower

abdomen. Gently rub in a downward circular motion. Do this just before retiring and the first thing in the morning (after your shower).

Cardamom Essential Oil

Cardamom was used at least 4,000 years ago. Add 4 drops of Cardamom Essential Oil to 2 ounces of warmed Macadamia Oil (Cold Pressed) or a carrier oil of your own choice. Gently massage a small amount on your lower abdomen.

Lemongrass Essential Oil

Lemongrass Essential Oil helps maintain healthy gastrointestinal function. That includes a variety of digestive problems – such as gas, stomach discomfort, indigestion, and flatulence. Add 3 to 4 drops of Lemongrass Essential Oil to 1 ounce of warmed carrier oil. Mix well and gently massage the lower abdomen.

CHAPTER THIRRTEEN

ETCETERA & ETCETERA

As with so many other things, there is always something more to say. The subject of essential oils is certainly among those. What follows is a short collection of all things essential oils.

<u>Essential Oil Remedy for Insect Bites</u>
Combine the following oils in a dark colored glass bottle with a stopper. Be sure the bottle has been sterilized.
    6 drops of Lavender Essential Oil
    8 drops of Cedarwood Essential Oil
    8 drops of Patchouli Essential Oil
    10 drops of Tea Tree Essential Oil
    6 drops of Geranium Essential Oil

20 drops of Eucalyptus Essential Oil
3 Ounces of carrier oil

Thoroughly mix the ingredients before each use. A technique my aromatherapist and teacher taught was to hold the bottle of oil in my hand for a couple of minutes before applying. This is a gentle warming of the oils.

The Wonderful Turmeric Essential Oil

Archeological evidence dates the use of Turmeric for medicinal and ceremonial purposes at least 4,000 years ago. Turmeric is said to support the immune system. It is used to improve the over-all quality of the skin and hair. It helps support the body's recovery processes from injuries and illnesses.

Add 2 to 3 drops of Turmeric Essential Oil to a diffuser to help lessen coughing associated with colds.

For those with respiratory issues Turmeric may offer some real relief. With 10 drops of Turmeric Essential Oil add the following essential oils:

- 6 drops of Ginger Essential Oil

- 6 drops of Eucalyptus Essential Oil
- 4 drops of Clary Sage Essential Oil

Mix these in a dark colored glass bottle. If you use this on your chest, be sure to add 4 ounces of Jojoba carrier oil and thoroughly mix. Do a patch test on a writst. If no problems show up, then take a couple of drops and gently rub onto your chest. Do this a couple times a day and especially just as you retire.

To use in a diffuser, add 2 to 3 drops, minus the Jojoba Oil. Sit in a room with the diffuser running and slowly inhale to bring breathing relief.

Moringa Essential Oil

Moringa, an important food source, is native to the country of India. Its high nutritional value makes it a very desirable plant. Its antioxidant qualities help protect one's cells from damage. It appears it has a positive effect on Asthma, Diabetes, Cholesterol levels, Constipation, and Headaches. Because of its long list of benefits, it is sometimes called "The Miracle Tree."

It is especially helpful to the skin and hair. Here is a recipe for fixing hair issues. You will need the following:

Ingredients

- 2 cups of a carrier oil. Be sure to get an oil that has excellent moisturizing qualities
- 10 to 15 drops of Moringa Essential Oil
- 5 to 10 drops Lavender Essential Oil

Directions

- Mix the oils together in a glass bowl or bottle.
- Apply to clean hair and gently massage it into the roots.
- Cover hair with a shower cap. Lave on overnight.
- Shampoo and condition hair as usual.
- You can also heat this mixture for a few seconds in a microwave, prior to applying. Some people like the

heightened scent that heating gives the oils.

Essential Oils and Inguinal Hernia

An Inguinal Hernia is experienced by abut 27 % of men; whereas only 3% of women experience an Inguinal Hernia. There approximately 899,000 Inguinal Hernia surgeries annually. Depending on the situation, surgery may not always be necessary. Specific exercises suggested by a physical therapist and approved by a medical doctor may help. The application of certain essential oils may reduce the need for surgery. The operative words here are, as always, check with you medical doctor.

Here is a essential oil recipe for an Inguinal Hernia. You will need the following:

Ingredients
10 drops of Cypress Essential Oil
10 drops of Lavender Essential Oil
8 drops of Frankincense Essential Oil
6 drops of Geranium Essential Oil

1 to 2 ounces of a carrier oil of your choice

Directions

Mix these oils in a dark glass bottle or if you don't have a small bottle, use a small sterilized dish. If you use a bottle, be sure its over is on tight, and sake the bottle for a full minute. If you use a small dish, be sure the object used as a stirrer, is also sanitized. Stir the oils until they are thoroughly mixed.

Make sure the mixed oils are slightly warm (hold the bottle in your hands for a couple of minutes or prewarm the dish before adding the oils)

Gently massage a couple of drops into the hernia area. Do this nightly.

AND ONE MORE

Embarrassing Rosacea

Due to their anti-inflammatory and anti-bacterial qualities, essential oils may help control the occurrence of Rosacea. It is estimated that 14 million adults in the United States harassed by Rosacea. So, what is Rosacea?

Rosacea is an inflammatory skin condition. Its symptoms include the following:
- Redness on the face
- Sudden flushing
- Sudden blushing
- Pimples
- Thick skin on the nose
- Blood vessels are visible

Several things may set it off. Among the triggers are the following:
- Sun
- Heat
- Foods that are spicy
- Stress

- Skincare products that are alcohol based
- Blood pressure medications
- Steroids applied directly to the skin

To help reduce the embarrassing redness and swelling associated with Rosacea these essential oils are recommended: Frankincense, Tea Tree, Chamomile, and Lavender.

RECEPI FOR ROSACEA*

<u>You Will Need:</u>

1 clean, sterilized 1-ounce dark glass bottle with stopper

45 drops of German Chamomile Essential Oil

35 drops of Manuka Essential Oil

Replace the stopper and shake until the oils are well mixed. Once this is done,

Take 12 to 15 drops and add to a carrier oil of your choice. Consider Jojoba or Tamanu Oil.

*If you like a sweeter scent add 2-3 drops of Rose or Lavender Essential Oil to the mixture.

Apply one or two drop to clean skin either in the morning or at bed time.

Thank you and Namaste
Norman W Wilson

Books by Norman W. Wilson, Ph.D.

Available on Amazon and other book stores

ABOUT THE AUTHOR

Norman W. Wilson holds two doctorates: one in the humanities and one in metaphysical humanism. He has certification in Aromatherapy and Essential Oils, Diploma of Distinction in Shamanic Healing/Energy Healing. In addition to over two dozen published books, he has dozens of articles published on the Internet, and two dozen videos on YouTube.

www.ingramcontent.com/pod-product-compliance
Lightning Source LLC
Chambersburg PA
CBHW070455100426
42743CB00010B/1627